THE COUNTRY WITH NO PLAYGROUNDS

Elena Croitoru

First Published in 2021
By Live Canon Poetry Ltd
www.livecanon.co.uk

All rights reserved

© Elena Croitoru 2021

978-1-909703-59-9

Cover photography:

THE COUNTRY WITH NO PLAYGROUNDS

Elena Croitoru is a British-Romanian writer and she has an MSt in Creative Writing from the University of Cambridge. She won the Charles Causley Poetry Prize and has been commended or shortlisted in the Edward Thomas Fellowship Award, the Wales Poetry Award, the Mairtin Crawford Award, the Winchester Poetry Prize, the Teignmouth Poetry Competition & other awards. Her first novel was shortlisted for the Wilbur Smith Prize - Best Unpublished Novel.

The Country With No Playgrounds is based on her experience growing up during Ceausecu's regime and the post-communist depression.

Acknowledgements

Many thanks to James Reed & my family, my tutors at Cambridge University's ICE, Exiled Writers Ink and all the editors and competition judges who have supported my work. A special thank you to Hannah Lowe, who has judged the Live Canon Pamphlet Competition.

'Tower Block Twelve', First Prize, Charles Causley Poetry Competition (judged by Lemn Sissay); *December Magazine*, Finalist Jeff Marks Memorial Prize (judged by Carl Phillips).

'Fish Bones by Candlelight', Highly Commended, Winchester Poetry Prize (judged by Andrew McMillan), Bridport Prize (Shortlisted).

'The Last Wedding', Second Prize, Teignmouth Poetry Competition (judged by Helen Ivory), Bridport Prize (Shortlisted).

'Playground', Second Prize, Edward Thomas Fellowship Award (judged by Jane Draycott); Commended, Cafe Writers Poetry Competition (judged by Zaffar Kunial).

'Things That Are Green', Highly Commended, Wales Poetry Award (judged by Katherine Stansfield); Shortlisted, Wasafiri New Writing Prize (judged by Malika Booker and Wasafiri editors).

'The Road to School No. 10', *Southword Journal*, Shortlisted, Gregory O'Donoghue Prize (judged by Brian Turner); *Best New British & Irish Poets 2019-2021*, Eyewear Publishing (judged by Nick Makoha).

'Tangerine', *The Interpreter's House*, Third Prize, Open House Poetry Competition (judged by Khairani Barokka).

'Hospital View', *America Magazine*, Runner-up, Foley Poetry Award (judged by Marjorie Maddox, Isabelle Senechal and Joe Hoover); Runner-up, Mairtin Crawford Award (judged by Moyra Donaldson and Naomi Foyle), Belfast Book Festival.

'How Far, How Far', *Solstice Magazine,* Finalist, Stephen Dunn Prize (judged by Reginald Dwayne Betts and Solstice editors); Bridport Prize (Shortlisted), Mairtin Crawford Award (Runner-up), Belfast Book Festival.

Contents

Playground

We grew up in our spare time,
beyond a tower block island
where pearly cement dust lay
over the nerves of nettle and bindweed leaves
which clung to the fractured, pale soil.

In winter, we would sink up to our chests
in snow and hide inside the unfinished body of a building,
its graffiti erased before it was written,
its three windowless walls wrapped around us
in an embrace that always stayed the same.

The place was empty, save for bone
fragments and jagged necks of green bottles.
We pretended this was a furnished room we owned
and thought God could not help us all
until later, and that when our turn came
we had to remember what we wanted.

We leaned against the concrete
which drained our body heat
through woollen clothes a size too small
until we could no longer bend our knees.

From this place we could not hear
the TV announcements that told us how
to love our republic, but we listened
to our silenced town and waited
to see if somebody could miss us.

Sinbad

After the shipmaster forgot them on the shore, Sinbad & his crew reached a palace
where a long table was set. A turkey lay on its back, its insides replaced
with mint, golpar & lamb. Sinbad refused to eat, but the other sailors couldn't stop
chewing until they slowly replaced themselves with mute beasts.

> My father took the last of the cold meat & put it
> on my plate. The fat lines the stomach, he said
> as he spooned red plum jam on his slice of bread
> & ate it. Then he went out & queued for hours
> in front of the general store, in minus twenty degrees
> weather. But he only came back with dead blue hands.

After his wife passed away, Sindbad was thrown into a communal tomb,
while still alive. He told himself, what is a grave but a bed in a dark, narrow room.
He had lost count of how many he had killed for their lavash & water. Days passed
before Sinbad could fashion some steps from the bones of the dead
husbands & wives. Then a fracture in the dark revealed a way out. Half sea, half sky

> We waited for the militia to knock on our door. Back then,
> they only came at night because the dark made everything
> clearer. My father counted how many times he had believed
> in our republic, though it was as imperfect as the sea floor.
> He said, after a certain point, the hunger stops
> you thinking, while showing your bones to the world.

To escape an island, Sinbad tied himself to the talons of a roc
which dropped him into a waterless valley, next to a carcass
whose skin had trapped the diamonds lying in the dirt.
But even when rich, Sinbad found his way to the sea again.

> I kept reading stories & waited for my father, though I knew
> we too had our dead, but their bodies bore nothing
> more than the impression of fingers
> from when they last embraced.

This is not an island, the shipmaster said before the singed whale sank
the sailors who believed they walked on land. Sinbad alone
held on to a plank & floated among waves as hard as cobalt.
Crystallised salt held his skin like a sarcophagus, until a merchant found him.

I heard the same warning, just as our city started crumbling.
Walking over rubble, my father returned, though
not as himself. Under layers of brick, I saw buildings I remembered
from another country long ago. I thought that maybe I never left
or maybe, I never got to where I was meant to go.

I saw Sinbad leaving the water for the last time, his feet cooled by the lacy seam of the sea,
& I said, come back Sinbad, you are me.

The Road to School No. 10

By then, our churches had been rebuilt
but God did not return.
The older communists retreated
into their flats and I would walk
under their balconies,
along fossilised pavements,
on my way to school no. 10.

Sometimes I would see a man,
naked from the waist up
or down, I can't remember.
He would macerate his arms
in liquor, then he would wave
and I would wonder
if my homework was good enough
to get me out.

Sometimes I would break
into the stadium that took
the loneliness out of our town,
and encircled it with wooden benches.
Its silence made me think
about the places we called home.

Sometimes I would run
into the girl who told me
not to laugh, before she showed me
her two missing knuckles.
I nodded because I knew
how that felt. Those bones were
the first things she noticed about me.

Sometimes I grew, not up but sideways,
building a new century city in my mind,
shedding the concrete skins of tower blocks,
putting up one glass panel after another,
so we could all see
what our country had done to our people.

The Last Wedding

That night was so dark that I could not find
my way out of it. My mother placed her Soviet-red
lipstick in an envelope purse while my father

lingered by the bathroom sink, his face half-eaten
by the dark, his scars like minute bullet marks.
The reflection in the mirror was yet another place

he couldn't run to. He didn't pack the toothbrushes & said
that when one is not allowed to return home
the desire to cleanse oneself disappears first. My mother

wore her cream wool cardigan though I knew
it wouldn't keep her warm in a bare concrete room.
She said my aunt would come if they weren't back

by morning. She looked out of the window
at the militiaman who watched our balcony
from below, the way one would watch

the funeral of someone still moving.
My mother put on low-heeled shoes
which glistened red, like the underlay of skin

because a body could only take so much
dancing. She looked at me as if forgetting
was the hardest way to live.

Pencil Case

The president had remade himself from paper
& watched us from his wooden frame,
demanding that love be taught. So we sang

for our country in navy uniforms
& ties as red as our frost-bitten hands.
When the bell rang, the teacher left us

so she could think for herself while we
remained at our desks. Our tender lungs held in
the fumes oozing from the diesel-imbued floor

& the smells of wet chalk & vinegar sponges.
One of the girls showed us a pencil case,
the type we couldn't find in small-town shops.

A glossy, padded box stencilled with pandas
& bamboo leaves, too unfamiliar to be real.
Inside it, a cracked parrot's egg, the kind

we wouldn't see for another ten years.
For a moment, we forgot about our president
& gathered around it, running our fingers

over the cream plastic compartments
of the pencil case, but really wanting
to touch the miniature egg,

just to feel the frailty of its cream shell,
while the dead bird inside it
rocked back & forth.

Fish Bones by Candlelight

For the third time that month,
      they cut the lights
in our street, as my mother laid a platter
      of fish on the table. We took out
the candles bought in churches
      that weren't meant to exist any more.
Under the shivering light, the cold
      blue-silver fish skins were seascapes.
Each bite of bland meat was spiked
      with dozens of fine bones, the salt
not enough to make it worth it,
      the white flesh falling apart into flakes as if
it never belonged to a living thing.
      The backbones were stitches on my plate
holding nothing together
      & I had figured it was just a game.
A bone at the right angle
      in the lining of my throat & I'd be out.
But it was hard to leave back then,
      someone was always watching
or listening as we coughed for breath.
      The dead eyes we set aside
with our forks, stared back at us
      while we took the bones, one by one
& restored skeletons on our plates,
      making it look as though we were
mourners by porcelain graves.

Hospital View

After they cut my father open
a fourth time, he lost a little more
of his life through the stitches in his skin
& I worried his soul had been out
for too long. A bag of blood dripped
along plastic veins, into his valves & atriums,
like an exposed, primitive heart.
He thought he was being replaced
with a stronger man, drop by drop.

By then he had more memories than flesh.
I asked if he was hungry & he said
his ration card filled out too soon.
But communism had ended years before,
though I still saw its geometric ghost
spread over the tower blocks beyond
the hospital's parking lot.

My father looked thinner, his skin unaccustomed
to the hollow underneath it. The new blood
stains on his pyjama top revived the old ones,
& made it look like God
had pressed a rose onto his chest.
He kept pulling his blanket to his chin, as if afraid
the seams of another world showed.

His eyes, caged by a mesh
of capillaries, were so far out
of his head, that I wondered if he lived
beyond himself. He kept looking down
at his hands because for many years,
his body was the only thing
he had owned alone.

If I visited too late in the evening,
it would take him a few moments
to remember me. He'd point
at the striated apples my uncle brought him
& tell me to eat, still trying to be
a father from beyond the edges
of his bed & asking
if I would come again.

The Stories My Father Told Me

The first one-eyed dervish sat on the stone floor
& told the ladies of Baghdad that the vizier
took out his left eye & placed it inside
his own empty socket. But what we see
with someone else's eye is never
to be trusted.

> There was nothing wrong
> with my father's sight except
> he saw our city the way it was
> before the revolution.
> Pristine, freshly sanded concrete,
> windows still dusted with ground
> glass, red socialist posters,
> balustrade edges sharp enough to cut
> a hand.

After an Efreet turned the second dervish
into an ape, he opened his mouth though
no one understood what he wanted.
It took one life for him to become a man
again.

> There was never a moment
> when my father wanted
> to run, he said as he sat
> in his bed, in the hospital ward,
> his back pressed against the iron
> bars of the headboard.
> He did his best when
> they changed the law or when
> they told him what to say
> though sometimes
> he could not remember
> which words
> he hadn't meant.

After his ship smashed against a magnetic rock,
the third dervish toppled the bronze horseman
guarding an island & killed the man
he was meant to kill. Sometimes the things
we're supposed to do lead us out
of ourselves.

From his hospital bed,
my father still remembered
the old communists taking over
the TV station, after they'd shot
the president & toppled the statues
in the Palace Square though
years ago, he'd said
he wasn't there.

Retrospective

The greenfinch stayed quiet
as it fed, soothing the frozen mud
with its unripe-lemon belly.
It must have noticed how silent
we had all become looking at it.

Its wings, the colour of white grapes,
fluttered until it flew over
the labour camp by the Danube canal.
I wondered if it would come back.
It must have noticed how skinny

we were though I knew the bird & I
had measured the winters
of each other's bodies differently.
Years later, after our nation buried
its revolutionaries & the cemetery,

like a flock of birds turned to stone,
became wider than our town,
another mute greenfinch
perched on my balcony
& I recognised its silence

because it made me feel
the same it did back then though
this time I was the one
who was eating. So I placed
a slice of seeded bread

on the iron balustrade,
thinking we were the ones
who did not kill to make
a living, but still made use
of the slaughter of others.

Tangerine

The day they came for him, I was given
a tangerine at school. He acted like my father, the way

people do when they think they made me.
I bit the glossy citrus skin, its oil

tasted like blood mist on my lips.
I thought our bodies have nothing

as soft as the linings of tangerines. They shot him
with machine guns while I ate

honey-laced watery flesh. Bullets spun
inside each organ like electrons,

tunnelling into his flesh until he fell.
The executioners would not forgive him

no matter how many times he died.
They pulled him by his hair

as I pulled white threads
from the empty tangerine heart so they

would not get stuck between my teeth.
I discarded the bullet-riddled peel

as they discarded him, not knowing
we would never leave his wake.

Things That Are Green

My memory of our concrete flat
has weathered to a green patina.
I rub it clean again then touch
the hand-stitched tablecloth my mother gave me.
My green fingerprints on the cream wool
resemble leaves that used to brush
against my window.
My mother refuses to remember them.
She cried too often when I was a child,
her breath a pallid green
plume on our third-floor balcony,
her hands as cold as the aluminium
lamp posts in our town.
I'd hold on to the hem
of her silk robe and look down
at dominoes shaped like tower blocks.
Cranes scratched the sky with metal limbs
and empty swings squeaked in the distance.
I used to wonder if my father could hear them
as he was made to crush
stones on the Danube canal,
unable to come back or speak his mind.
His face, as I imagined it, turned
a chimerical green. He was knee deep
in the river which wrapped around our country
                              and held it tight.

How Far, How Far

Our train moved faster until the Danube
was a blue fold in the horizon.
When our carriage fell off the dining table
you smiled with lips that had dried
as you queued in the snow
for monthly rations. That day,
you brought back the carcass of a bird,
laid it on the kitchen counter
& thought it was you, except
it had grey fat around the joints.
How far had it run
without a head. How far, how far
were we from each other though
coffined in a one bedroom flat.
The country outside had turned
into an abattoir with no silver tables
to rest on before we were meant to go.
Some days I would wait for you
thinking you laid down in the street
unable to get back up after they bruised you
all the way to your lungs.
You spent nights in the depot,
darkness dripping off you like oil,
diesel vapours clinging to your overcoat.
You watched trains departing from the same tracks
& wondered how far they went. How far
could I go, you asked of me every day
but there was no getting out,
father, you must have known.

Mechanical Frog

Years before the gunshots started
in the square, my father came back
after driving all night, his hands violet
and frostbitten. He brought
a mechanical frog in a cardboard box.

Spring morning green, watermelon red
painted on a fragile, Chinese steel body,
the first moving toy I ever saw. And when
I turned the key inside its metal heart,

it somersaulted with more life than any of us had,
letting out a croak from metallic lungs.
As usual, our town was quiet for miles on end
but our flat echoed with the clink of cogs
turning inside a small body

that leapt in all directions,
while my parents ate bread and home-made
quince jam for dinner without speaking.
The frog leapt again and again,
rehearsing life, better at it than most.

It felt no hunger and I could not open it up
to see how it worked because I needed it
alive. I placed it on the windowsill and it was startled
at the height of the tower blocks

and the emptiness of the concrete veins of our city.
I brought my ear close to the steel skin of the frog,
to listen to its pulse and almost didn't hear
                                        the gunshots.

Mother

It wasn't easy to find another mother
in our town where smoke only stopped rising
when it rained & pavements held water

which mirrored lime trees, making us think
we walked on glass & we could fall
into the pewter sky at any moment.

But one day we saw it, breaking
the horizon in two, its concrete body heavier
than our school building. On the radio

they said it could rebuild our country's limbs
& that it was the only thing we should believe in,
though its smooth walls looked unreal.

Iron bones held together its breastworks,
its rusted exoskeleton showed its age
& its cooling towers sprung out of the tired,

grassless ground like sun-dried phalanges
from a shallow grave. The air around it
could harden any skin & make eyes sting

so we became its stone children & watched it
petrify poplars & mullein flowers until
they were transformed into cement sculptures.

Silver steam burst out of its steel lungs,
& through its kilns, as though
all the clouds in the sky had been conceived

inside it. It swathed us in its cylindrical,
walls, inside a dense, chemical darkness,
while our limbs softened so much

we couldn't leave. Its sedimented silence told us
we were better off out there, where
stone-hard words couldn't lodge in our heads.

Tower Block Twelve

Tonight the piano on the fifth floor
falls silent as the militia dismantle it
to search for hidden notes. The pianist
tells them her musical score is a photo album
of sparrows on telegraph wires
& the electricity is about to slip through
the cracks in the sun-dried rubber.

Two floors up, a wild girl hides in a cupboard
with a jacquard curtain for a door while a chair
falls on the lino floor. A mother and a father
are being emptied out, so what they shout
to each other reverberates through
each hollowed ribcage & ties them
together the way barbed wire would.

A blue car ran over the man in flat 16
because a photograph of him leaving the queue for
milk proved that he'd wanted to defect.
But first they told him, an unexpressed thought
is easy to read if you watch someone for long enough.
The spider trapped in the man's suitcase
is starving but can't get out.

Next door, a retired teacher calls
the number to her son's flat over & over
but there's no answer & although she thinks
the militia know where he is,
they tell her nothing. So she bakes
a tray of challah bread as if
the dead could stave off hunger.

Time expands in flat 22, where the woman
who wants a divorce can't even find
happiness on her TV screen or in the lives
of her neighbours. She watches her husband
as he puts on a slick raincoat & she thinks
he is one of the informants
living in tower block twelve.

Next door, I wait for my parents
to come home & each time they do,
their footsteps are lighter as if
they'd lost something of themselves
& I think this means they would
shrink to nothing so each day
I have to weigh what is left.

Evacuation

They put the first saint on an oak plank,
tied ropes around its stone chest
& pulled him out of the church, though
when he slid on the iced tramline
& knocked himself against a wall, his fingers broke
& fell off like ordinary stones.

They immured Saint Peter, brick by brick
until his hard gaze could no longer
roam among them & when they finished,
they waited in silence & could hear
their own sins recounted
from somewhere inside them.

Saint Joseph fell facedown into the baptismal
font, so he was perpetually drowning
& because his skull broke against the stone
they didn't consider him worthy
of saving. All this while Saint Magdalen
kept looking down as if that could
stop the ground from opening up.

& when the workers stepped outside, their mouths
filled with snow as men in white coats
unloaded warm bodies wrapped in white sheets
from refrigerated trucks. From far away,
those men & women looked
like statues waiting to be saved.

Bucharest, 1989

The men slept on the pavement
& their boneless limbs were wrapped
around those next to them, as if
they'd wanted to embrace again

because they were never loved.
Only one man sank into the concrete alone,
while his fist rested on his chest
like a lump of old wax.

When my father found me
& pulled me into the warm crowd,
a bullet smashed the glass front
of an empty shop & it rained glass.

We crouched on the fractured cement
floor of a hollow tower block,
smelling the iron in the air, our backs
pressed against the bullet-ridden skin

of our city. The singed cotton wool sky
closed us in. A tank crushed
a plastic doll, her impossibly-clear eye
rolling in somebody's blood & a lock

of her curly hair stuck to the tracks.
We overturned the statues in the Palace Square
& that happens just once
in a few decades or however long

it takes to remember. Wake up,
some used to say, though
we'd been awake all along,
unable to run, but feeling everything.

Border

Our boat is made of ice though
my mother doesn't notice it,
even when her woollen gloves stick

to the oars. As the Danube flows below,
I wonder if they are watching us,
though we can't hide

in the still, pallid landscape. The banks
are covered in frost lacework
like the sides of a wedding veil worn

by a bride lying in a coffin. Cloudy ice floes
slow us down, clinking against our boat
& my mother keeps her winter sea gaze

fixed on the bridge we couldn't cross.
The ends of its balustrades finish abruptly
in the mist & the pikes that survive

in the deep hesitate before swimming under it
because some bullets always end up in the water.
The bottom of our boat is thinning,

becoming clearer, until it is like glass.
We try to steer it away from rocks
wearing masks of snow. I search the sky

for something that could pull us up
& all I see are static birds, like cuts
in a paper sky. When the water pulls

our boat towards the bank we are close
enough to see rotted autumn apples still
hanging on a tree trapped inside

an ice replica of itself & I think
this is what it means to not let go.
I want to tell my mother this

will never be the way home though
we all know at least one person
who wants to leave & we can't

stop them. I am not my mother yet
her thoughts belong in my head.
I would like to anchor our boat,

but the bank is now an impossible cliff
& the river is getting wider until it becomes
                                    the sea